# VALLEY WALKERS

# VALLEY WALKERS

MARILYN PAULL YARNELL

Publishing services by Selah Publishing Group, LLC, Tennessee. The views expressed or implied in this work do not necessarily reflect those of Selah Publishing Group.

ISBN: 978-1-58930-229-7
Library of Congress Control Number: 2009900295

# Dedication

This book is dedicated to family and friends that have gone on before.  The light that radiated from them while they were on this earth made it very easy to follow.

I thank the Lord for their wise counsel and guidance.

Keep watching Guys…I'll be there!

# MANY THANKS...

Once again, I thank my lovely Aunt Mavis Paull, who devoted many hours reviewing my manuscript, and for offering me her very sage advice.

And I want to thank my cousin Susan Paull Scott who also took her precious time to read and edit the manuscript. So much good input from these ladies, I felt very honored to be so blessed.

And last but not least, I will always give thanks for my Christian parents, Rev. Lyle M. and Ethel M. Paull, who raised me up in the way I should go.

Thank you Jesus.

# CONTENTS

# INTRODUCTION

I thought I was in the throes of a Spring Cleaning fit when I decided to tackle a closet recently, but I was to soon realize that it was the prompting of the Holy Spirit that directed my path.

Buried under books on a top shelf was a large mailing envelope that I had completely forgot about. Its contents were tablets and loose papers, work that I had done years ago. There were the beginnings for the 'Dear Simon" letters. Pages and pages of scriptures on various topics for praying the Word. Stories and thoughts I had forgotten about, and wondered if I had written. Prophecies and poems and dreams.

Some material had been used in "Daughters of Zion." Other material set aside because it didn't 'fit'. When "Daughters" was finished I had cleaned up my mess by putting everything left over in the envelope and 'stored' it in the closet. But God had a better idea. He returned me to the closet.

He began to deal with me on several subjects until I started to see the basis of another book. How exciting! Like a puzzle it took awhile for all the pieces to fit into place, but here it is.

Little did I dream then that one day He would have me share my thoughts with the whole wide world (it's a little like opening my diary), but if my stumbling and mumblings as I made my way up the ladder going from Glory to Glory will help someone else find their path, then so be it.

Within these pages are life lessons from myself, family and friends, people who shared what they have learned as they walked through their valleys. And in so doing bring the comfort whereby we are comforted to you, the reader.

So from my little corner of the world I share my thoughts. It's not perfect, but then neither am I. But in the words of that dear man who's in heaven today, Pastor E. V. Hill, "This ain't it. We're just going through."

Eternity awaits!

> *Lo, I am with you always, even unto the end of the world. (Matt. 28:20 KJV)*

# THE CIRCLE OF LIGHT

In the dream I was as a huge spectator, looking down upon the scene before me. To my right was a high balcony with a railing. The Lord God was reclining along its side and it was as though He was reading from papers in His hand.

Below me I saw myself standing on a small mound in a circle of light, not unlike a spotlight circle. Beyond the light was darkness.

Surrounding me in the darkness were demons, lots of demons, stretching out their hands trying to grab me. They couldn't penetrate the light, and I knew that as long as I stayed within that circle of light they could not touch me.

But I was also 'stretched out'. I was reaching towards heaven, beseeching God for help.

Then, my Father God looked over the balcony railing.

And He reached down His mighty hand and lifted me up out of all my troubles.

Praise the Lord forever!

> "...the Lord looked down from His heavenly sanctuary. He looked to the earth from heaven." (Psalm 102:19 NLT)

# ONE

*Hear, O Israel: The Lord our God is one Lord (Deut. 6:4)*

*There is one body, and one Spirit, even as ye are called in one hope of your calling: one Lord, one faith, one baptism, one God and Father of all. (Eph. 4:4-6)*

# HE COMFORTS US

*All praise to the God and Father of our Lord Jesus Christ.*
*He is the source of every mercy and the God who comforts us.*
*He comforts us in all our troubles so that we can comfort oth-*
*ers. When others are troubled, we will be able to give them the*
*same comfort God has given us.* *(2 Corinthians 1:3-4 NLT)*

# MY MOTHER LAY DYING. . .

ETHEL MAY CLEMENT PAULL, Born Nov. 1913, Died
March 2006

> *Her children arise and call her blessed (Proverbs.*
> *31:28)*

Barely 5' tall, for 92 ½ years she had walked through this
life. And for 99% of those 92 years she had done that upright.
She was truly blessed. And so were we.
She had faithfully served her husband, her family, her
Lord. My father left us for his heavenly home 10 years
earlier and mother was indignant. He wasn't supposed to
go first.
For 65 years they had stood by each other, richer or
poorer, in sickness or health. So, at 82, without him, she
had no purpose.
She refused to leave her home, and because we all lived
within shouting distance we let her stay. She loved her
flowers and her garden and kept herself busy.
And she talked to Daddy.

The decline was slow, mentally before physically, but it was there.

Still she refused to be moved, so we decided that as long as she wasn't a danger to herself or others we would leave her be.    Finally she could no longer work in her flowers nor keep her garden, but Daddy was still there.

And she could still talk to him…and did.

I prayed the bloodline around the property, and kept Angels busy protecting her from dangers seen and unseen. But Time was the enemy.

The little strokes that finally felled her intensified the dementia, and although the hospital wanted to put her into a nursing home, I refused and brought her to my home…at last.

I'm not going to dwell on the obvious.   Anyone who has taken care of a loved one under those conditions knows the hardships.    Suffice to say the Lord knew what I would need before I did.

To begin with, my granddaughter and her husband were staying with me temporarily while he worked in the valley.   When I brought Mom home my granddaughter was there to help, and when her husband had to return to their home, my granddaughter stayed, along with my two great grand babies.

Without her I could not have cared for Mom by myself. It was a huge blessing.

Many a time in the middle of the night I had to get Lyndsey up to help me get Mom off the floor and back into bed.

Many the time during the day when she was 'restless' we parked a baby in her lap and instantly the old mothering instincts took hold and she was occupied and quiet, cooing and soothing for both.

It was amazing to watch.

She wanted something to do to "help me." I had a pile of old towels that I used for rags. Shaking them out I piled them in her lap and told her it would be a big help if she would fold them for me. Because she was always the perfectionist, she was occupied for quite a while, but satisfied that she was 'helping'. The truly funny thing about it was that she never asked again for something to do.

But there were some truly miraculous happenings that the Lord allowed me to witness in the final weeks of her life. And it's those that I want to share with you.

Along with everything else Mom had 'Sundowners'. She slept very little at night and very little during the day. She would go from room to room looking for Daddy.

So at night, before she became bedridden, to keep her confined to her bedroom I had to use a baby gate. She would prowl her room, empting drawers and the soap bottles that Hospice brought, anything else that came to hand ended up in odd places.

One night after putting her back into her bed I sat down on the side and held her hand.

"Mom," I began slowly searching for the words, "your body is old and sick. It's not going to get well. You need to turn your mind to going home to Heaven, to Daddy. He's waiting for you there. Think about him. Keep him in your mind. Just let go and go to him."

Mom lay back on her pillow and I tucked her in. She never said anything but closed her eyes and relaxed onto sleep.

As usual, the first thing in the morning I checked on her. As I entered her room she opened her eyes.

"Well," she said, in a surprised tone of voice, "I didn't expect to be here this morning." And then rather indigently, "And who was that man that stood at the foot of my bed last night?"

"Was it Daddy?" I ventured.

She shook her head negatively. But I knew.

Several years earlier she had a kidney infection that went into her blood. She was very, very sick and we almost lost her then. When she got home from the hospital she began to tell us how upset she had been with the woman in the next bed. It seemed the lady had visitors one night and a man had stood on the other side of the curtain and stared at her.

"For the longest time," she continued, "he just stood there and stared at me." He had glasses, she remembered.

We knew it was Daddy, even though she didn't recognize him. He was on the other side of the veil, watching over his beloved.

Mom's ability to walk or move deteriorated very rapidly after that night. She became bedfast and 'frozen'. It was so painful for her to move herself that we had to keep changing her positions.

Late one night about a week later I heard her mumbling. I couldn't make out what she was saying so I sat down and leaned my elbows on the bed. The position she was in made speech difficult to understand but there was something…something….

As I watched her, and listened, the reality dawned.

She was 'talking' to someone.

Physically she was in her bed, but spiritually she was on the other side.

She was behind the veil.

She was animated.

She would laugh.

Her face was glowing.

As she talked her little boney hands were moving.

Then she would be quiet as though she was listening to someone.

She would respond and laugh and talk and listen for more than two precious hours.

I heard the word 'Lyle' several times as she addressed her husband.

I heard 'Ralph' very plain, her brother's name.

I heard "you're making the wall too high," and very clearly, "shovel" and I had to laugh to myself. She's already got Daddy digging up her garden.

It was an experience I'll never forget.

How comforting to know we're so close. Just behind the veil, in the Holies of Holies, where God dwells, our loved ones dwell as well.

After she quieted and slept, I crept to my own bed, aglow with the presence and the peace of the Lord. Later in the night I awoke and heard her 'talking' again, but this time I only smiled to myself and went back to sleep.

I knew where she was.

And I knew how happy she was.

And I knew it wouldn't be long before they would be together again forever more.

> *Therefore, since we are surrounded by such a huge crowd of witnesses to the life of faith, let us strip off every weight that slows us down... (Heb. 12-1 NLT)*

A letter to my Aunt on the occasion of the death of one of my Fathers younger brothers and a dear uncle, **NILE BENJAMIN PAULL** (Born Aug 1919, Died July 2004)

Dear Aunt Leone,
Susie, Nancy, Molly, Jean, and families.

What can I say that hasn't been said already. He will be missed by all of us.

I always wondered what the Bible meant when it said, "death has no sting."

When Charlene* died so suddenly, the Lord told me that she was ready and I saw her standing in a golden field. From that time on I didn't spend a lot of time grieving. Death had no sting.

When Daddy* was dying I kept telling him to let me know when the Angels were coming. The night he died I fell asleep on the couch next to his bed. I had been awake over 24 hours and I was exhausted.

Suddenly I awoke! He was gone.

Only 45 minutes had passed. But I know that I know that I know he shook me on his way out to let me know that the Angels had come. Death had no sting.

Oh, I miss him. And it doesn't take much thought to bring tears to my heart, but I cannot grieve. He's in Heaven with Jesus.

For years now I have seen the death of a loved one as a tear in the fabric of the family. At first it is very large and hurtful. But as time goes by the hole gradually fills in and the hurt abates. It will always be there though, because even as the hole fills in it leaves a scar, a rough spot. It's always noticeable, and if you just rub your finger across it…the memories surface.

Our family has a lot of scars in its fabric, some bigger than others, but none as new as this one. And it will be a while, a long while, before it fills in. But there's no sting, because he is in Heaven with Jesus.

The Bible says in Ecclesiastes, "There is a time for everything...A time to be born and a time to die...A time to cry and a time to laugh...A time to grieve and a time to dance."

Once again this family has entered into a grieving time. But not without lots of wonderful memories of a man who made people laugh and sing. Who made music* and memories for at least three generations, maybe four.

Because of Mom's frailty we cannot be there to hug you, and to honor his memory. But know that we are of one Spirit, and we share our thoughts and love with you all.

You are in our prayers...

*My sister, Charlene Carol Paull Graham (Born Feb 1935, Died March 1992)

*Rev. Lyle Miller Paull (Born April 1911, Died February 1996)

*The Paull Family Hoedowns were of legendary stuff. Family and friends would come from miles around bringing their instruments and song books, (Yes, we even had a Paull Family Songbook). A few quotes from a poem my Uncle Nile wrote can only give you a glimpse...

## THE BANJO PICKER

"And after they'd finished their supper,
     and a wondrous potluck was consumed,
Someone said, "Well, its time for a hoedown,
     And the instruments all to get tuned!
And out came a couple of banjos!
     A fiddle appeared on the scene!
A harmonica and a guitar,

And they started to look like a team!
And there followed a Paull Family Hoedown,
    As happens each Christmas with Joy!
And they played, and they sang Christmas Carols,
    Till the time came to pass out the toys!"

"And we'll thank the dear Lord for those memories,
    For they softened and filled up our hearts,
And brought us all closer together,
    And made us sad being apart.

And there's gonna be more reunions,
    And hoedowns we're still gonna hold,
Cause hoedowners and banjo pickers,
    Make memories that's spun of pure gold!"

# THE MASTER BUILDER

*In my Father's house are many mansions… (John 14:2 KJV)*

My Mothers brother and another dear Uncle, Ralph Harold Clement (Born Feb 1912, Died Jan 1995) worked hard from the age of 15 learning all aspects of building from all the jobs he held.  In 1935 he built his first house for his new bride.  All totaled he would build six houses for his family (plus several boats).  He loved the Lord and read his Bible daily.  He was strong in his faith and his life was his witness.  When it became hard to read he played Bible tapes and listened to Christian radio.

Within the last year of his life my Uncle had a dream. The dream which came to a painstaking builder of six houses was a dream of a building so beautiful that it had to be in heaven, he told his family. He had never seen anything like it on earth. It was so beautiful that he said words couldn't really describe it but that it had to be built by a Master Builder; the craftsmanship was far and above presently known skills. He was made aware, he said, that this was prepared for those that love the Lord.

This dream uplifted him and he knew it was a preview of the glory that was awaiting him.

Can we not all take solace in the beauty that awaits us? As beautiful as this earth is, we know that it is only a type and shadow of the glory beyond.

> *Eye hath not seen, nor ear heard, neither have entered into the heart of a man, the things which God hath prepared for them that love Him. But God hath revealed them unto us by His Spirit; for the Spirit searches all things, yea, the deep things of God.(1 Corn 2:9-10 KJV)*

## JACK'S DREAM

My elderly Uncle might not have been able to describe the wonders he saw but not so with our family friend Pastor Jack Davis. Early in the morning of January 21, 2007 he found himself walking in Heaven with his dog Toby. So in his own words....

"I saw a big, BIG house on top of rolling hills that were all covered with grass. The color of the grass was the deepest, greenest and most beautiful I'd ever seen. And being a farmer I have seen my share of green grass.

This was undeniably the biggest house I had ever seen in my life. I could put our whole house in just one room and have plenty left over. I noticed a big, big window that completely surrounded the house

Next thing I saw was a little old bald man* and he invited Toby and I inside this huge house. I don't know if I went through the door or not, but suddenly we were inside.

The man said "This is your house." And then I heard the music. Beautiful singing and worshipping, and the house, inside and out, was full of God's Glory and Light. The music was like nothing I have ever heard or seen in my life! It was glorious worship and praise that seem to be coming out of every wall throughout.

I thought to myself, "Sierra* has never heard stereo like this." It was so glorious! I was overwhelmed by the majesty of it all. The Glory and Light was very bright and peaceful and there was such an atmosphere of love. So much love!

I said to the little man I was with "Where do you buy furniture and appliances to furnish this big house?" (The house was absolutely bare with no furniture at all.)

The little man answered very casually, "You will figure it out," and He just disappeared!

The next thought that went through my mind was, "We need throw rugs in here." And as I thought 'throw rugs' they instantly appeared. And it connected. Thought – prayer – speak.

Mark 11:22-24 *"Have faith in God," Jesus answered. "I tell you the truth, if anyone says to this mountain, 'Go throw yourself into the sea' and does not doubt in his heart but believes that what he says will happen, it will be done for him."* (NIV)

Then I noticed the floor. It was the most beautiful wood grains and colors. Toby went running down the long hall and suddenly stopped. He came to a halt on a throw rug and dust was boiling up all around him. I though to myself, "Darlene* is not going to like all this dust. I need to clean it up."

And then I thought..."How am I going to do this?" Again Mark 11: 22-24 – thought – prayer – speak!! And instantly a big, BIG dust mop appeared. So I started down the hall.

I looked down and now the floor was not hardwood but pure marble. The clearest and deepest marble I've ever seen. It looked like water, but it was marble. It looked like it was 6" deep with marbling thrown in it. If I would look down the hall past where I was walking that floor looked like hardwood. But under my feet it was this marvelous marble.

As I went down the hall with the dust mop in hand I saw that it was not 'dust' at all but pure gold dust. I've never seen gold dust that pure – ever! I used to pan for gold in Ashland, Oregon so I know what I know about gold dust.

I thought...Boy, this place is bare. We need furniture in here. Suddenly all the rooms I could see had furniture in them. It was completely furnished with beautiful furniture. Thought – prayer - speak!

Next thing I looked at was those windows again. I've never seen windows like this in all my life. They did not have window casings. It was one continuous window.

I wondered to myself how one would put up drapes on windows like that. Again, Mark 11:22-24. Thought – prayer – speak. Instantly the most beautiful drapes and hangers I've ever seen. They were purple and white. And I have never seen purple like that purple before. I can only describe it as heavy and full. And the white was not like our white. This white was deep and so rich and full.

Next I told Toby, "We need to find the bathroom." So we went looking. To my amazement there are <u>no</u> bathrooms in Heaven.

Toby and I walked into a big room. Ahead was a long, long table. On this table were lots and lots of books. Make a note: there are no light switches in Heaven either or light fixtures because of the Light and Glory of God. Remember the light that lit up the inside and outside of the house was the Glory of God and Jesus!

Back to the long room and the books. I walked up to the table and opened up one of the books. Its pages were not paper but like very thin stone. There was writing on these stone pages and I began reading. It spoke of all the dreams and visions that I had over my entire lifetime that the Lord had given me.

The next book I looked at was a book of all the prophecies I have been given by the Holy Spirit speaking through me over my lifetime. This Scripture came up through me.

Malachi 3:16-17. *Then those who feared the Lord talked with each other, and the Lord listened and heard. A scroll of remembrance was written in His presence concerning those who feared the Lord and honored His name. "They will be mine," says the Lord Almighty, "in the day when I make up My treasured possessions. I will spare them, just as in compassion a man spares his son who serves him." (NIV)*

We are Hs jewels!

His treasured possessions!

As I was standing in that house I was looking out of the windows. I was looking at the beautiful rolling hills and the beautiful green grass and being a rancher also I thought "What a place for cows and calves." (Remember Mark 11:22-24 thought – prayer- speak)

Instantly before me was the most beautiful herd of Black Angus pure bred cows and calves you've ever seen. They were eating the grass and it never got any shorter! No matter how much they ate the grass stayed the same height.

I thought, "They need water," and immediately the water gushed out of the ground. It flowed through the grassy field. As the water flowed rocks instantly appeared to make a channel as far as I could see.

I looked and looked and believe me there was no cow manure in sight anywhere in that field!

* Jack believes the 'bald headed' man was Elisha (2 Kings 2:23 KJV)
* Sierra Capps, a great granddaughter who lives with them.
* Jack's wife Darlene

> For we know that if our earthly house of this tabernacle were dissolved, we have a building of God, a house not made with hands, eternal in the heavens. (2 Corinthians 5:1 KJV)

# SISTER EVELYN

Sister Evelyn Friday Knootz, a true servant of the Lord God and my spiritual mother, lay dying. Her daughter and son-in-law (Jack and Darlene Davis) were at her bedside singing hymns and praying when Jack had a vision.

He saw the heavenlies. Not our heavenlies, but God's. The colors were magnificent, deep, rich hues, beyond anything we could think or see.

And then…he saw it. Floating serenely, sparkling like diamonds, and coming down from God the Father, a beautiful white gown.

"Mom," he whispered, "I see it. It's coming. I see your wedding dress. It's so beautiful. It's like nothing you've ever seen."

She had been in and out and he didn't know if she could hear him. But, he said, she smiled and by the next day, she was gone.

She went into Glory, the Bride of Christ, wearing a wedding dress that was designed and made especially for her, a Designer Original, ready for the Marriage Supper of the Lamb.

Thank you Lord for honoring this wonderful woman of God!

*And the Spirit and the bride say Come. And let him that heareth say, Come. And let him that is athrist come. And whosoever will, let him take the water of life freely. (Rev 22:17 KJV)*

# ALL DOGS GO TO HEAVEN. . .RIGHT?

And last, but not least, what about our furry friends? Haven't we all taken solace that some day maybe we'd see them in heaven? After all, the Lord is coming on a white horse, so there must be animals in heaven, right?

When my Spiritual Mother laid to rest her beloved dog Blue, she wrote a beautiful poem honoring Blue's life. But it's the last few stanzas that I want to share with you.

# THE GOLDEN CROSS

So that night the Lord gave me a Vision.
Amid our tears and grief we had finished our mission.
And to comfort our hearts He showed me a door.
I went to open it to see what was in store.
I looked and saw a bright green grassy lawn and trees.
And there I saw that glowing right before me
Was a beautiful, beautiful Golden Cross,
Standing about two and a half feet tall.

I was so thrilled, I was at a loss.
To think God was showing me this gorgeous Cross.
And then I saw it was covered by flowers of gold.
It was so beautiful, and my eyes did behold
Small flowers entwined in a violet hue
Among the gold, and I knew
It represented my beautiful, beautiful Baby Blue.
"Good bye my Blue"....
Her Mama

*Blessed are those that mourn. They will be comforted. (Matt 5:4)*

# AS I SAT BEHIND THE VEIL

I was only about three years old when Papa came into our bedroom one morning and told my older brother and me that the Doctor had brought us a baby sister. And as he carried me into the adjoining bedroom where Mama lay with this baby sister cuddled in her arms, I'm sure that I must have been thrilled within my childish soul.

All told my Mother bore eleven children. All were born at home and all cuddled close to a loving Mothers heart as if each might have been her first.

I had the wonderful privilege of being born into a Christian home. Though our family was large there was always love enough to go around. Through all the years of childhood, youth, and then the years since I was grown, I had never heard my parents quarrel, or speak harshly to one another.

But the joy that was mine on that morning when my Father showed me the new baby sister was soon to turn to sorrow. Six weeks later little Maxine was dead. Some kind of an infection my Mother told me when I was old enough to understand. I can still remember as if only yesterday how still and pale she was as she lay in the new black bed that had been placed in our bedroom. And as she was carried out of the house I can still remember that I wondered why they were taking her away from our home. To young to know the answers though not to young to wonder why.

I am fifty years old now and I have been in the homes of loved ones when that last breath was drawn and the stillness of a lifeless body told us that another soul had gone. Through the years I had searched for the answer to the question that was mine when I was only three. I had often wondered…would the words so softly spoken in the

home or at the funeral bring the answer?  As they sat behind the veil would their questions all be answered?  And
then one year ago I received my answer as my own Father
passed away and I was brought to the moment when I too
would sit behind the veil.

Did others hear when words were spoken?
    Or when we tried to console?
Just what was their deep reaction?
    Could we help their grieving soul?

Did you ever stop and wonder
    As some soul you tried to cheer,
If the words that you were speaking
    Were the words that they would hear?

I never could this question answer
    Until my Father passed away.
And now while I was grieving
    What would others have to say?

My thoughts were not around me
    On this day or in this place.
For my anguished heart was aching
    To see my Fathers face.

And my thoughts went back to childhood
    Many memories to assail.
And I don't know what was spoken
    As I sat behind the veil.

Rev. Lyle M. Paull (1911-1996)

# IN MEMORY
# OF OUR DEAR FRIEND LYLE

In the land of no returning
    there stand one so "fair" today.
And he walks and talks with Jesus
    (never being very far away).

Sometimes he stands in the Valley of Angels
    praising God for all His victories won.
While on earth he prayed, "Jesus, I love thee,
    For I know thou art God's only Son."

They say in the Valley of the Lily's
    Jesus died across the sea.
And Lyle now stands a witness
    for one and all to believe!

For he had beheld God's Glory
    and he is walking hand in hand
With his Lord and his Redeemer
    Through that Golden Promised Land!

Good-bye our dear friend Lyle…for only a moment or two, and we will all be with you. You were always such an inspiration to us.

This was written in February 2006 by close friends Jack and Darlene Davis, and Michael and Evelyn Koontz, in honor of my Father's, the Rev. Lyle M. Paull's, home going. Thank you dear ones.

> *Precious in the sight of the Lord is the death of His saints.* (Psalms116:15 KJV)

# TWO

Two great lights, the sun and the moon, at creation (Gen 1:16)

The two cherubim on the Ark of the Covenant (Ex 25:22)

The Ten Commandments were written on two stones (Ex 31:18)

The disciples were sent in pairs (Matt: 10, Mark 6:7)

Two to witness the great tribulation (Rev. 11:3)

# OLD PHOTOS

I have a picture in my mind. One that will never go away. A photograph, if you will, of a time and place forever gone.

I see fingers.

My father was a laborer all his life. From the time he was a boy old enough to hold a hoe and milk a cow he worked by the sweat of his brow. The second eldest in a family of eight surviving children, his own Father away most of the time, he held responsibilities that most children in this day and age would never guess at.

And the picture? His finger. A big finger, hardened and callous, cracked and strained, being held securely in the grip of his first great grandchild just a few days old.

A contrast of dark and light, hard and soft, old and new. A bond.

Suspended in space and firmly etched in my mind is a pure, pink, tiny hand firmly grasping his old, stained finger as though this beautiful little newborn he now held in his big hands sensed the love and protection that was available to her for eternity.

I wonder if she felt the love from this giant of a man. I wonder if she could sense that here was a man that would move heaven and earth to protect her.

How much more our heavenly Father.

We have a heavenly father with hands that formed the worlds, made man, slew giants, and moved mountains. Work hardened hands extended to us.

"Take my hand", He begs. "Give me your burdens. Trust me and I will make a way where there is no way. Follow me, and I will forever direct your paths. Love me, and I will give you life everlasting."

Extend your hand. Grasp His finger. Don't let go.

*For He is our God.  We are the people He watches over, the sheep under His care.  (Psalm 95:7 NLV)*

## EVERLASTING ARMS

A friend and co-worker had to take a business trip to Florida.  She was not real fond of flying and was grousing about it one morning at work.

Suddenly in my mind I saw an immense Jesus standing beside the earth and just above His outstretched arms an airplane was flying.

"Tell Patti," He whispered to me, "that underneath are the everlasting arms."

God is faithful and ever mindful.  He knows our thoughts and He knows our comings in and goings out!  Even when we're not thinking about Him, He is thinking about us.

*The eternal God is your refuge, and His everlasting arms are under you.  (Deut. 33:27 NLV)*

## CAN YOU PRAISE ME?

The first time I heard the voice of God, and knew it, was when Mike (my oldest son) was 11.  He had completed the Hunter's Safety Course and for his birthday his father bought him his first gun, a rifle.  He bounded into the house, full of excitement, waving his prize.

Bubbling over with enthusiasm, his mouth going forty miles an hour, he laid the gun across the arms of the chair next to the sofa where I was sitting and raced back outside. I must admit I felt none of his excitement, and with a lot of reservations I eyed the gun.

*"Can you praise me?"*

The voice came from deep within, yet I heard it with my ears. I sat very still, hardly breathing. There was no doubt in my mind whose voice I was hearing.

Again, *"Can you praise me?"*

"Yes Lord," I whispered, "I can praise you. I put this gun in your hands. I know you will take care of my boys."

From that day to this, I have never worried about my sons and guns. They hunt a lot, and there are accidents every year in the woods, but I know that I know that I know God is taking care of them. The Angels are surrounding them. They are in His hands.

Praise the Lord!

> *He who fears the Lord has a secure fortress, and for His children it will be a refuge. (Proverbs 14:26 KJV)*

# BOULDERS

My Father was a mountain man. From a young man he worked in the lumber industry. At first he worked in a sawmill and then hauling the lumber to town.

After we moved to the valley he went to work in the woods, setting chokers, driving logging trucks, running loaders, falling timber. As a cat skidder he not only pulled the logs out of the woods but built the roads that the truckers used to move the logs down out of the mountains. He loved the mountains, so when the Lord gave him this dream it was very special to him.

"In the dream I was taken into the mountains. The trees were large and tall. The dark green needles high in the branches made a blanket of shade on the small bushes and plants beneath them.

Scattered among them were Vine Maples and Dogwoods dressed in their autumn finery. A few clouds drifted aimlessly in the sky. O, the beauty of it all!

And then I heard the call of a mountain stream. Soon I was standing on the bank looking into the clear, cold water.

The water was flowing fast as if it were late for an appointment. Rocks, some small, some large were in the stream bed, all restricting the flow in various degrees. As I stood drinking in the beauty my thoughts wandered to other mountain streams and as I thought about them I was made to remember that they all had many rocks and boulders in them.

And then as the Lord was showing them to me I saw in my spirit a fast, flowing stream without the stones. What a difference the stones made. Without the stones the water flowed fast and clear but it lacked the color and beauty.

Then the Lord showed me that the mountain stream I stood beside was made beautiful because of the obstructions in the stream bed. For here the water bounded off the rocks and instead of being colorless and still, it sparkled and glittered like a million little diamonds.

The Lord spoke to my spirit and said, "This is like the lives of my people. In the stream bed of life they flow silently and colorless towards a dry lake bed. But then a few pebbles appear and causes a few sparkles, then larger rocks which cause more brilliance. The more rocks in the stream bed, the more beauty is manifested. The water is slowed down in its flow and the brilliance of the risen Christ is seen by many."

*And He said unto me, My grace is sufficient for thee: for My strength is made perfect in weakness. Most gladly therefore will I rather glory in my infirmities, that the power of Christ may rest upon me. (2 Corinthians 12:9)*

I first found the poem. But when I came across the actual narrative I decided to use it instead. However, I was torn between the beauties of the two of them, so instead you get both!

## BOULDERS

In a dream, I was taken to the mountains
    And there I saw the trees.
I saw the trunks and branches,
    I also saw the leaves.

I saw the bark upon the trees
    That protects them from the cold.
I saw the young trees growing strong,
    I also saw the old.

I saw them in the spring and summer.
    I saw them in the fall.
I saw them in the winter time,
    When they had no leaves at all.

Then I saw a mountain stream.
    It was as clear as glass.
No obstructions in the stream bed
    And it flowed swiftly past.

But then I saw some boulders
    And the stream began to change.
It struck the boulders with a mighty force.
    It roared as if in pain.

But through the battle that took place
    Twixt the boulders and the stream,
There came forth an eerie beauty
    And another chapter of the dream.

The Lord showed me that in our lives
    As they flow swiftly past.
They remain quite colorless
    Quite like a pane of glass.

Then in the stream bed of our life
    There's a boulder in our way.
Now I might have tried to go around,
    But I heard my Savior way:

"If you want some beauty to shine forth,
    Hit the boulders in the face.
Never choose to go around,
    You are held in my embrace."

Rev. Lyle M Paull
1911-1996

# WHY ME, LORD?

Jesus is my Lord, my God, and I do not understand why God loves me so. What is man that thou are mindful of him?

I do not understand why He has chosen to bless me among women. Am I not as a flower in the field that fades and dies?

I walk with an anointing on my head, and I do not understand why He has chosen to put it there. Am I not as the grass that writhers?

I love my Lord, my God, my Jesus. I walk with my hand in His. He goes before me, protects me with His love, His power, His presence. He removes from my presence those enemies who come against me, come against His will for me.

He hears and answers my prayer.

He is my healer.

He is my provider.

He is my all in all.

I do not understand why He does so much for me because I do not always behave according to His word.

As we walk along, I'll see something that turns my eye, and I'll dart off after the glimmer. It's all too easy to slip off the Spiritual level and drop down to the human plane.

And yet, I'm not alone. He never forsakes me. He never leaves me.

Only now, He is behind me and I am 'facing the wind'.

The full force of the wind strikes me, because I have gone ahead of my Lord.

Still He is patient.

He waits...tapping His foot.

I run back to His forgiving arms and we turn away. Now He's going before me, and we walk again towards the goal.

He loves me even though I have weaknesses, and short-comings. He holds my hand. And when I slip, I never hit the ground, for He holds me up.

He sits beside me at night and cradles me in His arms. He comforts me, sings to me, and talks to me.

He keeps me. He cares for my family, leads them, heals them, teaches them, and saves them.

I have done nothing to warrant all this attention from a God so high.

But Jesus has. He went to the Cross for me. And through the Blood of Jesus, God sees me, and therefore sees His son, whom He dearly loves.

He has become my Father.

I in Him.

I have become His child.

He in me.

He loves me. He blesses me. He has patience with me. He protects me. He goes before me.

I love Him, and I will serve Him all the days of my life.

Even so, Lord Jesus, come!

Amen

*No height, nor depth, nor any other creature, shall be able to separate us from the love of God, which is in Christ Jesus our Lord. (Romans 8:38-39)*

# HE CARES

As Jesus walked the shores of life
His footsteps led to me.
I had built myself a wooden boat
and just pushed out to sea.

So quietly He stood
and watched with tearful eyes.
He knew of an approaching storm,
tho yet...a cloudless sky.

He didn't say a word to me.
He knew I wouldn't hear.
For on that day I was on *my* way.
I had no thought of fear.

But darkness settled o're the sea,
and the storms of life did blow.
I became lost in the dark of night.
I knew not where to go.

But Jesus knew the plight of me
And thru the night he came.
And since He turned my boat around
I've never been the same.

Then Jesus took the oars from me
And He began to row,
All fear then left...within was rest,
for He knew which way to go.

Take Jesus into the boat with you
Let Him your pilot be.
When storms assail you need not fear
for He will calm the sea.

Rev. Lyle M Paull
1911-1996

# OUT OF THE BLUE

At the age of eighty my little bitty, skinny Mom had a heart attack. It was completely unexpected and the Doctor called it 'old age and worn parts'.

I was at work when the police called. Apparently she had walked to the store and was on her way home. She was only a block away when she realized she was in trouble so she stepped into the local butcher shop for help. He was kind enough to lay her down in his office and call 911.

I reached her before the ambulance took her away so taking her hand I told her to keep repeating the Name of Jesus, and not to worry, I would pick up Daddy and meet her at the hospital. When we reached the hospital they had already taken her into the emergency room and wouldn't let us go to her. So we waited...and waited.

I cannot ever remember sitting down to a meal without hearing Daddy give the blessing. It was the standard 'Thank you for this food' prayer, so when I heard someone preach years ago on sanctifying the meal based on the Priests sanctifying the utensils that were to be used in the Temple it stayed with me. Looking back on my actions that day, it's the only thing I can think of that made me act as I did when they finally let us go to her.

I wheeled Daddy into her room and saw with dismay that she was all 'hooked up' to bags containing I knew not what. She lay still and white, and cracked a small smile as she saw us coming.

Without even thinking about it I reached out and grab bags in both hands. "I sanctify the contents of these bags in the Name of Jesus for the health and healing of my Mother."

The Doctor turned and looked askance at me. Mom smiled and Daddy nodded. It was done.

She recovered nicely and after a few days came home to live another 12 ½ years.

God blessed us, blessed His Word, and was faithful to perform it.

Praise His Name forever!

# TO A MRS. OSWALD

I had delved into a box of pictures intent on sorting and putting them into albums when I found the following. There was no date on this poem, hand written on two small pieces of note paper in my Fathers handwriting, but it was addressed to a Mrs. Oswald.

# A SPECIAL PRAYER

O God of love…
My heart goes out tonight to one whose life is shattered.
My love goes out to one alone whose heart is torn with grief, to one who stands alone…forgotten.

To one whose heart is bleeding, whose soul is scarred because of the sin of another.

To one who tried but failed before the judging eyes of men.

To one whom this night sits alone with tear stained face.

To one whose name shall ever be repeated on the lips of man, not in love and honor, not in praise, but in condemnation.

This one to whom my heart cries out is the mother of a boy gone wrong.

A young man who from his youth was led in devilish ways…possessed by Satan…and now his final deed is done and Satan laughs.

And a mother cries…

And sits alone.

O God, this is my prayer, that thou will guide her safely to thy throne.

O God of Love, abide within her soul and let her hide her sorrows and her grief within thy care.

And in this trying hour where she stands so alone before the eyes of man, though judged she be and guilty found, I pray O God, that just a drop of crimson blood fall from the Cross and touch and spread and cover every hair upon this Mother's head,

And so anointed cause her to find that there is One, yes One, who doesn't look the other way, but claims her as His own forever and a day.

Amen and Amen.

*Faithful is He that calleth you, who also will do it. (1 Thessalonians 5:24)*

# POINTING TO THE SKY

It was a freak accident.  I was leaving my office building when the wind caught the heavy metal door and slammed it shut upon the end of the index finger of my right hand.  Blood was everywhere.  I could only grab some tissues out of my purse and head for the hospital.

The hospital was kind enough to stitch it back together and wrap it so it looked like a football and tell me that I had to keep it 'pointing to the sky' and dry!

Because I am right handed it was a major inconvenience.  In my position as Business Manager, there was a lot of typing, bookkeeping, and computer work.  It was hard to turn the key in my car, take a shower, brush my teeth or even comb my hair, let alone eat!  I had to keep the finger elevated to keep the blood from rushing to the end and throbbing, which meant that I had to sleep, or try to sleep, with my finger pointing upwards.

So it was with a major case of 'feeling sorry for myself' that I walked into the local post office a few days later.  Naturally, after eyeing the bandaged appendage 'pointing to the sky', the clerk asked me for the particulars which I gladly shared so he could share in my misery.

He nodded and said very matter-of-factly, "A lady in our branch office slammed three fingers in the safe the other day, and they had to work the combination before she could get them out."

Wham!  Nothing like knowing there is someone else worse off then you to pop your bubble of self-pity.  Major lesson learned.

Its human nature to think that what we are going through is ours alone. It can be so dramatic in our minds that we tend to turn inwards, curl up like a sow bug (my great grand babies call them rolly polys) and nurture our hurts, lick our wounds.

But there is nothing that we go through that is not common to man.

And God is faithful. He can use everything, no matter how big or small, to help someone else if we let him. Even smashed fingers.

> *But remember that the temptations that come into your life are no different from what others experience. And God is faithful. (1 Corinthians 10:13 NLV)*

# THREE

*For there are three that bear record in Heaven, the Father, the Word, and the Holy Ghost: and these three are one.(1 John 5:7)*

*For as Jonah was three days and three nights in the belly of a huge fish, so the Son of Man will be three days and three nights in the heart of the earth (Matt: 12:40 NIV)*

In His personal ministry Jesus raised three people from the dead. The son of the widow of Nain (Luke 7:11-15), the daughter of Jairus (Luke 8:41-55) and Lazarus (John 11:43-44)

# PRAY THE WORD!

One day I was meditating on the following scripture, "...so is My Word that goes out from My mouth; it will not return to Me empty, but will accomplish what I desire and achieve the purpose for which I sent it," (Isaiah 55:11 NIV).

I thought why not take it one step further than simply repeating it out loud back to the Lord, why not write a 'legal paper'. Now I most certainly am not an attorney, nor have I ever worked for one, so I used my imagination and created one with lots of 'whereas, therefore and inasmuch'. But this is serious stuff, an agreement between you and God Almighty. If it's all His words, how can He not take heed?

So what is an agreement or covenant?

The word covenant as a noun means...

-Dictionary

1. An agreement, usually formal, between two or more persons to do or not do something specified.

-Bible

2. The conditional promises made to humanity by God, as revealed in Scripture.

-Law

3. A formal agreement of legal validity, esp. one under seal.

So here's something new and fun and entirely scriptural. How easy it is to pray the Word when you can get your hands on some Pocket Promise books or a good concordance. Here's an example:

*Father, in the name of Jesus*, we agree that your word is true and amen.

Acts 16:31 says, *"Believe on the Lord Jesus Christ and thou shalt be saved and thy house."*

John 14:14 assures us that, *"if you ask anything in My name, I will do it."*

1 Timothy 2:4 tells us that *"God who will have all men to be saved, and to come unto the knowledge of God."*

Matthew 18:19: *"That if two of you shall agree on earth as touching anything that they shall ask, it shall be done for them of My Father which is in heaven."*

Therefore, in Jesus' Name, we consider the salvation and deliverance of _____ as done according to your word and will.

From this day forward we shall praise your name for, *"The Lord redeemeth the soul of His servants."* (Psalms 34:33)

And because, *"whatsoever we bind on earth is bound in heaven"* (Matthew 18:18) satan, in the Name of Jesus Christ of Nazareth, the son of the living God, we notify you that according to this agreement you are bound on this day and hour, and from this time forward in _____life. He/She is covered by the blood of Jesus and surrounded by the Angels of God, and satan you will not function or operate, harass or hinder him/her in any way from receiving their inheritance. We hereby render you helpless in this matter.

Therefore, because *"in the mouth of two or three witnesses shall every word be established"* (Matthew 18:16), we hereby set our signatures as a means of releasing our faith.

Dated this _____day of _____,____

_____
Witness

_____
Witness

It is important to have someone agree with you and sign with you. (Matt: 18:19-20). I had my wonderful spiritual mother, known to many thousands of people as Sister Evelyn Friday during her lifetime, pray over these with me and sign them. In the Name of Jesus we declared it done and amen!

Now go to it! Wherever you want victory in your life, household salvation, finances, companionship, healing, or a deeper relationship with God, seek out the Word, the promises, and return it to the Lord.

Here's another one, (albeit it's a little long):

**In the Name of Jesus Christ of Nazareth**, the son of the living God, and as my privilege as a child of God, I come boldly before the throne of grace to make my request known unto God according to Thy Word.

**WHEREAS:** Your Word tells me to, *"Call unto Me and I will answer thee." (Jeremiah 33:3)*, and *"Behold the Lord's hand is not shortened, that it cannot save; neither His ear heavy that it cannot hear." (Isaiah 59:1)*

**WHEREAS:** *As Jesus is my high priest, seated on the right hand of God and ever liveth to make intercession for me (Romans 8:34,) who is able to save to the uttermost (Hebrews 7:25), who will be merciful to the unrighteous (Hebrews 8:12), and by the blood of His cross reconcile all things unto himself (Colossians 1:20)*

**WHEREAS**: *Jesus came into this world to destroy the works of the devil(1 John 3:8), and therefore thou hast put all things in subjection under His feet (Hebrews 2:8), and upholdeth all things by the Word of His power (Hebrews 1:3)*

**WHEREAS:** *God which cannot lie (Titus 1:2) promised to deliver us from every evil work (2 Timothy 4:18), for the grace of God that brings salvation hath appeared to all men*

(Titus 2:11), and our Saviour Jesus Christ, who gave Himself for us, that He might redeem us from all iniquity (Titus 2:14), for the Lord God knoweth them that are His (2 Timothy 2:19).

**WHEREAS:** Jesus Christ came unto the world to save sinners (1 Timothy 1:15), we both labor and suffer reproach because we trust in the living God, who is the savior of all men (1 Timothy 4:10), who will have all men to be saved, and to come unto the knowledge of the truth (1 Timothy 2:4).

**WHEREAS:** Thus saith the Lord, ask Me of things to come concerning My son, and concerning the works of My hands command ye Me (Isaiah 45:11), the desire of the righteous shall be granted (Proverbs 10:24).

**WHEREAS:** For I am the Lord. I shall speak and the word that I shall speak shall come to pass; it shall be no more prolonged; Thus saith the Lord, there shall none of My words be prolonged anymore, but the word which I have spoken shall be done, saith God (Ezekiel 12:25 &28).

**WHEREAS:** No good thing will be withheld from them that walk uprightly (Psalms 84:11). They that seek the Lord shall not want any good thing (Psalms 34:10). Behold the days come, saith the Lord, that I will perform that good thing which I have promised (Jeremiah 33:14).

**WHEREAS:** My covenant will I not break nor alter the thing that is gone out of My lips (Psalms 84:34), Because I have spoken it, I have purposed it, and will not repent; neither will I turn back from it (Jeremiah 4:28).

**WHEREAS:** No weapon that is formed against thee shall prosper. This is the heritage of the servants of God (Isaiah 14:17). And having spoiled principalities and powers, He made a show of them openly, triumphing over them in it (Colossians 2:15).

**WHEREAS:** To proclaim the liberty to the captives and the opening of the prison to them that are bound (Isaiah 61:1). There is no power but of God (Romans 13:1).

**55**

**WHEREAS:** *All things are of God, who hath reconciled us to Himself by Jesus Christ, and hath given to us the ministry of reconciliation; that God was in Christ reconciling the world unto Himself, not imputing their trespasses unto them (2 Corinthians 5:18-19)*

**WHEREAS:** *Whatsoever you do in word or deed, do all in the name of the Lord Jesus, giving thanks to God and the Father by Him (Colossians 3:17) and, whatsoever you shall ask in My name, that will I do, that the Father may be glorified in the son. If you shall ask anything in My name, I will do it (John 14:13-14).*

**WHEREAS:** *We, having the same spirit of faith, according as it is written, I believed, and therefore speak (2 Corinthians 4:13), for we walk by faith, not by sight (2 Corinthians 5:7), and being fully persuaded that what He had promised, He was able also to perform (Romans 4:21).*

**WHEREAS:** *Thanks be to God, which giveth us the victory through our Lord Jesus Christ (1 Corinthians 15:57); now thanks be unto God which always causes us to triumph in Christ (2 Corinthians 2:14).*

**WHEREAS:** *That if two of you shall agree on earth as touching anything that they shall ask, it shall be done for them of my Father which is in heaven. For where two or three are gathered together in My name, there am I in the midst of them (Matthew 18:19-20). And this is the confidence that we have in Him that if we ask anything according to His will, He hears us. And if we know that He hears us, whatsoever we ask, we know that we have the petitions that we desire of Him (1 John 5:14-15).*

**WHEREAS:** *As we recognize that we wrestle not against flesh and blood, but against principalities, against powers, and against the rulers of darkness of this world, and against spiritual wickedness in high places, (Ephesians 6:12); and that we cannot enter into a strong man's house and spoil his goods,* *except by first binding the strong man (Matthew 12:29); there-fore, whatsoever we shall bind on earth shall be bound in heaven, and whatsoever we shall loose on earth shall be loosed in heaven (Matthew 18:18).*

**WHEREAS:** This is the petition we desire. That dated this day ____of _____.__, we proclaim _____to be delivered out of bondage, and that he/she come and abide under God's canopy of love, and receive his/her salvation, thus fulfilling the word of God to His children. In the Name of Jesus Christ of Nazareth, the Son of the living God, we bind satan and all the spirits operating in the life of _____, to keep him/her out of the kingdom of God. Satan, you are bound and you'll not keep him/her from being loosed from the powers of darkness.

Therefore, in the Name of Jesus Christ of Nazareth, the Son of the living God, and in the mouth of two or three witness shall every word be established, so we set our sig-natures this day to release our faith.

Dated this ____day of _____,__

_____
Witness

_____
Witness

**57**

# IN A BATTLE...?

Sometimes we have to get out a big stick. But no one has a bigger stick than God! Remember, it's His words!

Father God, in the Name of Jesus, we accept that your word is true and amen.

Isaiah 55:11 *"So shall My word be that goeth forth out of My mouth; it shall not return unto Me void, but it shall accomplish that which I please; and it shall prosper in the thing whereto I sent it."*

Therefore, we stand in agreement concerning our children.

Isaiah 49: 15 & 18 (NIV) *"For the Lord has comforted His people and will have compassion on them in their sorrow...For all your children will come back to you. As surely as I live, saith the Lord, they will be like jewels or bridal ornaments for you to display."*

Isaiah 49:24-25 (NIV) *"Who can snatch the plunder of war from the hands of a warrior? Who can demand that a tyrant let his captive go? But the Lord, who says, the captives of warriors will be released, and the plunder of tyrants will be retrieved. <u>For I will fight those who fight you, and I will save your children.</u> I will feed your enemies with their own flesh. They will be drunk with rivers of their own blood. All the world will know that I, the Lord, am your Savior and Redeemer, the Mighty One of Israel."*

Isaiah 54: 16-17 (NIV) *"Your enemies will always be defeated because I am on your side. I have created the blacksmith who fans the coals beneath the forge and makes the weapons of destruction...But in that coming day, no weapons turned against you will succeed. And everyone who tells lies in court will be brought to justice."*

Jeremiah l: 19 (NIV) *"They will try but they will fail, for I am with you and I will take care of you. I, the Lord, have spoken."*

Zephaniah 3:14 & 19 (NIV) *"Sing, O daughter of Zion; shout aloud, O Israel! Be glad and rejoice with all your heart, O daughter of Jerusalem! For the Lord...will disperse the armies of your enemy. And the Lord Himself, the King of Israel, will live among you! At last your troubles will be over, and you will fear disaster no more.*

*And I will deal severely with all who have oppressed you. I will save the weak and helpless ones;*

We sign our names in agreement this _____ day of

_____, ____.

_____

_____

Now that you have the idea, take it and run with it. I guarantee you that satan will fight! But you can laugh in his face. Recognize the battles that seem to come out of nowhere for what they are...and stand. The victory is already yours, and satan is a liar! A *finished* liar!

# THE PLAGUE OF FLIES

My Mom and Dad had flies!

Well, not in the sense that they were surrounded because of malodorous body odor, but of their location next to a dairy farm and across the road from cow pastures.

When Mom and Dad purchased their second home in the early eighties in this sleepy, rural valley they did not know that in order to fertilize the fields and get rid of their 'stockpiles of stock piles', the dairy farmers would liquefy this product and literally shoot it through their special equipment onto the pastures, thereby bringing every fly that could walk or 'fly' to check out the new cuisine. Have I sufficiently grossed you out?

And it wasn't just a few here and there. They were literally crawling in droves out from under the eaves, and from around the window frames. We could only surmise that the attic and walls were breeding grounds of unsurpassed proportions. Think Si-Fi Channel.

As I was into the 'whereases' and 'inasmuches' at the time I decided to see if I could apply the Word of God to the fly population.

**BECAUSE** we are Blood Covenant people, in the Name of Jesus we state God's Word is true.

**INASMUCH** as the Lord severed the Land of Goshen in which His people dwelt in the day of the plague of flies, that no swarm of flies will be found there, that He actually created a division that no fly could penetrate (Ex. 8: 21-23) that they may know that God was in control over ALL things,

**INASMUCH** as Jesus was the Sacrificial Lamb once and for all that made permanent the atonement for the Children of God that there be no plague among them (Num. 8:19),

**INASMUCH** as we have made the Lord our refuge and our habitation, we claim the promise that no evil shall befall us, neither shall any plague come nigh our dwelling (Ps. 91:10),

**INASMUCH** as Jesus said, "If ye shall ask anything in my name I shall do it" (John 14:15),

We recognize that the flies swarming at our home in Myrtle Point is contrary to the Word and will of God for His people.

Therefore, in the Name of Jesus Christ of Nazareth we hereby rebuke them and order them off the property. They cannot stay nor can they return.

According to Matthew 18:19 we set our hands in agreement and consider this enforced by our Father in Heaven.

Dated this _____ day of January 1983.

Signed_____

Signed_____

We prayed over it and Mom and Day signed it. (I still have the original signed version.)

Both Mom and Dad are gone now so I cannot ask them directly, but I can honestly say that from that time until they sold their place some 10 years later I never saw or heard of another infestation like I witnessed that day. My oldest son Michael and his family lived in the house full time for about two years and he never saw it happen during his time there either.

The farmers were still fertilizing their fields but our 'Land of Goshen' was severed from the plague!

Folks, the Word works! Whether it originated 4,000 years ago or thirty! The Lord God (the Word) is the same yesterday, today, and tomorrow!

Praise the Lord!

# AND THE LORD SAID...

### GOD APPROVES...

*My daughter, even as you made out these contracts, even as you have been abiding under the shadow of the almighty, even as you have put your hand upon these contracts, even as a firebrand out of the fire, there is a brand of the Holy Spirit upon you, saith the Lord.*

*I am the same God yea, this night that is showing forth My power. I the Lord God will not let you down. Have Faith in God and know of a surety that this is coming to pass. For again I say unto you, I did speak to you and I have said this to you, just to abide.*

*Abide in the shelter of the arms of Jesus. Abide, for as you are doing this, as you are abiding, you are doing this as unto Me through faith, saith the Lord.*

# ACROSS THE VALLEY

As I looked across the valley at the city on the hill,
the beauty and the peacefulness just caused my heart to thrill.

And I knew the Lord was looking down, and living in my heart, for only He can give us Peace...with Him is where it starts!

As I looked across the valley at the city on the hill, I could see the cattle wend their way to fields by the Coquille.

Their days work now was ended, their nights work just begun, like us, they can't quit working with the setting of the sun.

As I looked across the valley at the city on the hill, the lights began to twinkle as the eventide grew still.

Then faintly 'cross the valley came the ringing of a bell, telling me God's in our Heaven…and all is well!

All is well!


By Nile B. Paull (1919-2004)

My uncle penned this poem 6/28/81 as he sat on the front porch of Mom and Dad's Myrtle Point home.

# FOUR

*"For by Him were all things created: things in (1) heaven on (2) earth, (3) visible, and (4) invisible, whether (1) thrones or (2) powers or (3) rulers or (4) authorities: (Col. 1:16 NIV)*

There are four seasons; spring, summer, fall and winter.
There are four points on the compass: north, south, east and west.
There are four elements: air, earth, fire and water.
Four horsemen of the Tribulation (Rev. 6)

# IN THE GARDEN

My name is Mary Magdalene, and I have come to the garden alone. It is very early in the morning and the first rays of the sun are breaking over the Eastern hill. The rays shine on the roses and the dew is sparkling like diamonds.

A soft breeze whispers, as if to tell a story yet unknown, the greatest love story the ages will ever know! It is a soothing sound...like musical notes borne on the breeze...ever so gently blowing, much like the memory of my Savior's voice as he would speak to me!

I hadn't always heard the voice that stirred the hearts of men. I was a prostitute, steeped in sin, an outcast from the flow of decency. Even Simon shook his head in unbelief as I came into his house while Jesus sat at meat. (Luke 7:36-50)

I poured oil on the feet of Jesus as Simon groaned within that Jesus would allow it, though he, himself, had on numerous occasions slipped through the shadows in the night time to my door, there to spend countless hours in my embrace. It's all past now...for Jesus came and in His sweet way condemned me not, but rather filled me with His love.

But these have been frightening days as the Chief Priests in Jerusalem (out of envy) have condemned to a death on the cross the one I love so dearly. Jesus turned my life around, and so now I am in the garden to anoint His body with sweet spices, a token of my love.

BUT SOMETHING'S WRONG!
WHAT HAS HAPPENED?
HE ISN'T HERE!
THE TOMB IS EMPTY!

My heart cries out, my body trembles. My knees give way and I fall to the ground. I do not know how long I was there until... *He spoke*...and the sound of His voice was so sweet that even the birds stopped their singing!

Again my body trembles but this time for joy. Tis Jesus speaking, "*Mary...Mary*". And the joy we shared, as I tarried there, no one has ever known.

Then as His love once again surrounds me, I cry out, "Rabboni...My Master!"

*©1984 REV. LYLE M. PAULL (1911-1996)*

**Dear Simon,**

Five years ago you showed me a door. "I love you," you said. "Stay here. I'll keep you safe. I'll protect you." So I moved in...into the basement of your life.

For five years I lived in the basement of your life. Not because I wanted to, but because you put me there. It was necessary to protect me, you said, because, well...you were married and she didn't understand you. You loved me, you said, so you hid me away.

At the beginning I saw you quite often. My joy was full. I was content. But then, as time went by, your visits became less and less.

I tried not to notice. I made excuses for your absence. And then you'd come and I'd fling open my arms, and it was like you'd never been away.

And then you would leave.

Shut the door.

And I would sit in my darkness, quietly crying.

As time went on I stayed there...in the basement. And even though you came and went, I waited there.

Quiet.

Making no noise.

No waves.

From time to time you remembered me and would stick your head in the door.

"Are you still there?" you would ask. Yes, I was still there.

Always there.

Your stability.

You counted on me to be there. You needed me to be there. So, I always was. Always ready to welcome you with outstretched arms, with love and forgiveness. You romped and played, and did your thing, secure in the knowledge that I was 'there'.

I began to hear other noises outside the door. Dust began to filter down through the cracks. I tried to ignore it. I didn't want to believe it.

I wanted to trust you, to believe in you.

Then I found a window, and I looked out as through a lattice, darkly at first. Gradually I began to see you in the twilight, in the evening, as darkness was falling over your life.

I saw you with another woman. She was dressed as a harlot. Sly and cunning, but turbulent and willful, her feet stayed not in her own house.

Her man was not at home.

She looked for you.

She found you.

And with much justifying and enticing arguments she persuaded you with the allurement of her lips. She led you along. She perfumed her bed, and promised you consolation and delights. Suddenly you yielded and got caught in her net.

And that cost you more than you had to give.

In my grief I stumbled around searching for the way out. I found a stairway. There was a light at the top. Slowly, painfully, I began to climb.

But still, every once in a while, you opened the door.

"Are you still there?" you would ask.

"Yes" I would cry, and run to meet you, eagerly welcoming you back into my arms.

Forgiving.

Loving.

But then you would leave, and the darkness would fall again.

I stumbled around until once again I found the stairs.

One step at a time.

Through bitter tears.

With a broken heart.

Wanting to die.

Slowly, painfully, step-by-step, I climbed the stairs again. Suddenly I discovered I was not alone, a hand reached out for me.

A steady hand.

A helping hand.

But then you came and once more I ran back down the stairs to your arms. Pouring out all my love upon you. Hoping you would stay this time. But you would leave again, and I'd fall to the floor.

Crumpled.

Broken.

More pain than I could bear.

But now, in my place on the floor, I found a hand reaching down to me, picking me up, giving strength to my legs and leading me back to the stairs.

Gradually I made it to the top. Conquering each step was a hard battle, but now I see clearly. I'm basking in the warm glow of a new love.

My Savior's love.

He loved me before I knew Him.

He came down in my pit and lifted me out, because He loved me.

Things are different now. Another door was opened. I saw another light. I went to it and found someone who was waiting *for me*.

I had to climb a steep stairway, but now I'm on the top floor. I'm no longer 'bargain basement'.

I am a designer original.

Top floor merchandise only.

I can't go back to the basement. And, I really don't want to. If you want me you must come up to the top floor, and pay a great price.

Yes, I still love you, but it's different now.

So please...

Please...

Come up and meet my Jesus.

He loves you too.

With love,
Mary M.

PS: I am going to pray for you

# AND THE LORD SAID:

**TAKE MY HAND...**

Oh my daughter, saith the Lord, I have looked at you through a veil of many tears. I have looked at you and I have seen your crucified heart. I would tell you now that I am lifting you up, even though you think I'm not.

I have lifted you up many times when you have been discouraged. But now the Hand of the Lord has literally come and lifted you up into a high place, because I have so much for you to do, saith the Lord.

There are many people that you will help. There will be many stars in your crown because of your friendships and faithfulness. So take courage.

Behold! Take courage! For all this time I was molding you and shaping you into the image that I would have you to be. For I promise you, the latter part of your life will be a whole lot happier and much greater than the first part, saith the Lord.

**I WILL LIFT YOU UP...**

I will lift you up as you are being still. Be still before me and I will nourish you. I will mend your broken heart, saith God, and I will let you catch a new vision of your Lord.

In the meantime, I am leading you and guiding you in ways that you shall go, saith the Lord. I am not going to part from you. Even this day I am going to bring a peace into your heart, as you trust me.

And yea, as you relax before the Lord I am going to be with you.

I will speak special, precious things in your mind and heart, saith the Lord.

### LOOK UP, SAITH THE LORD...

Yea, just look up for I am God that is with you. I say to you that I have seen all your heartaches, and I have bottled your tears. I am the Lord God that will defeat these devilish things that are binding you and hindering you. I will give you the desires of your heart, saith the Lord.

I will answer your prayers for this is a new year, and a new day is dawning for you, saith the Lord. You will feel the arms of your God around you, and I will lead you and show you what to do.

### I SEE YOU...

I see in you a broken heart and a broken spirit. But in my word I said a broken heart and a broken spirit I will not despise. I will comfort you and console you for I am taking up the broken pieces, saith the Lord.

I am making you a vessel of honor to your God, for you are not a quitter. Yea, you are hanging on to your God. You are hanging on to your God and the Lord is putting in your heart a determination to serve me, more than you will even know, for you are truly bringing your requests to your God, saith the Lord.

### I HEAR YOU...

The Lord your God hears and answers prayer, and is seeing these things, for the Lord God lives and reigns forever, saith the Lord.

You will look back and see that the broken pieces that are being mended are going to be for your benefit in the days to come.

Be not afraid but trust in your God, for this time is a momentous time in your life for all the changes that are going to take place. I am not dead but I am alive, and I am your God, saith the Lord.

### *ANGELS SURROUND YOU…*

I have you in My loving arms. Even now you are surrounded by legions of Angels. You will come into greater victory, saith God.

Yea, you will feel My loving presence and the Angels of glory will be leading you into the happiness that is your inheritance even on this earth, saith the Lord.

### I AM NIGH…

I am nigh unto you. I am close to you tonight. I am here beside you to bless you, saith the Lord.

Angels are around about you, encamped around about you. You cannot see them, but Angels are there beside you to undertake for you.

I am the Lord God that has been with you this day in a real manner to love you and encourage you, to bless you, to answer your prayers, and to be with you, for the victory is yours. Even to the end of the world I will hold my people close to Me for you are as in a school, and I am the Lord God that is teaching you, saith God.

### *THE POWER IS IN YOU…*

Yea, know this. The power that I used to create the universe, even so abides within you! Therefore, let it come forth, and you shall see that the flowers shall bloom.

Even though it is wintertime, it shall be as springtime. New life shall come forth from you. Yea, and there shall be buds upon the trees. Yea, and blossoms shall come forth, saith the Lord.

I see in you a new progress. You have come forward another step.

Behold! You have heard me, and you have moved in spite of the circumstances.

*Yea, behold! I come to you now, and I bring forth new life within you, new strength within you. Your health shall spring forth. You shall see that the weariness is gone, saith the Lord. Behold! The heavy load has been lifted. You shall rejoice, and great joy will come to you.*

*Yea, and behold! What you have not even thought possible and imagined, the Lord brings to you, and you shall know that God has done this thing, saith the Lord.*

> *The Lord is nigh unto all them that call upon Him, to all that call upon Him in truth. (Psalm 145:18 KJV)*

# FIVE

*"Therefore I take pleasure in (1) infirmities, (2) in reproaches, (3) in necessities, (4) in persecutions, (5) in distresses for Christ's sake: for when I am weak, then I am strong."* (2 Cor. 12:10)

Five Levitical offerings (Lev. 1-5)

Five barley loaves (Matt. 14:17)

Five wise virgins (Matt. 25:2)

**Oh Simon!**

What is this that you have done, my love?

What have you done to earn the displeasure of God?

He is the Lord God yea, that looks upon mans heart, and He has looked with displeasure at your heart the last few days…"with great displeasure, saith the Lord."

It is the Lamb of God that stands by me. He loves me and bought me with His blood. "Therefore," saith God, "What man should come and degrade my children, and thereby degrade the Spirit of the Lord that is in my children…causing them hurt?"

Simon, there is a great need for you to get your life straightened out, and God has been dealing with you. But God says you have a great stubbornness, a stronghold of satan. He says you have a handicapped version of what you should be.

The Lord would say to you…"seek His face and draw back from your ways." Seek the face of the Lord, and receive of the Lord, and be set free, for you need deliverance. He wants you to become a whole person, and not lean on man's understanding and teaching.

But it is a man's will that comes against the working…and the perfect will of God being formed.

No, I'm not perfect…but neither am I to be hurt and treated so carelessly. It is God Almighty who protects me, and your foolishness has earned His wrath.

You have my forgiveness…now seek His. Stop letting satan dominate you. Your self-righteousness is as filthy rags.

God will bring you out of the hog wallow…like the prodigal son. Would you go back to it?

He will greet you with open arms…would you now spurn Him?

He will put a robe of righteousness on you...would you lay it down for your own robe of self-righteousness?

He will give you a gold ring of eternity...would you shed all these things in favor of your own doctrine...or man's?

God is not deceived...but you have been...by satan...and you have let him take your goods.

Turn around Simon...while there is still time.

God loves you, but He is an all consuming fire...and you are playing with fire.

Sincerely,
Mary M.

PS: I'll always pray for you

# AND THE LORD SAID:

### COME AWAY WITH ME

*My beloved, come away with Me into the high places, saith the Lord.*

*My beloved, come away with Me and I will be unto you a lover, a friend, a mother. All things I'll be unto you.*

*Today I would comfort you. I would be your comforter. I would keep you warm. I would keep you from any drafts. I would keep you in My loving arms, saith the Lord.*

*Therefore cast your care upon Me today. Cast all your dreams upon Me. For it is written that I said, "Bring your burdens unto Me and leave them there." Therefore, bring your burdens to Me now and leave them with Me for I am able, saith God.*

*I am the one that is more than able to undertake every one of your burdens, in order to bring forth your life into being what it would be.*

*Cast your care upon Me today and look to the Lord your God, and you shall see it come to pass that I have moved for you in strange and wonderful ways, even that you know not of right now, for I am leading you and guiding you, saith the Lord.*

### I WILL ANSWER YOUR PRAYERS

*I will give you the desires of your heart. For it is written in My word that I will give My people the desires of their heart. And the Bible is true and faithful, saith God.*

*There are great things in the future that you cannot see right now. You are looking as through a mirror, a dark mirror, and you cannot see plainly. But I see, for I am on the other side, saith God.*

*Behold! I will show forth My power to you and answer your prayers, for I see the heaviness of your heart, and your discouragement in this hour, but this will all turn around. For I am going to glorify My name and do mighty things and you will see and know that it is the Lord, saith the Lord.*

### EVEN AS LAZARUS...

*I see your broken heart, and I never despise a tear. Nor do I ever condemn a broken heart, but rather that is the time that I am full of compassion. I am full of love, and full to overflowing to the place that I immediately start to work to bring comfort and solace to your heart, saith the Lord.*

*Many times I have told you many promises. There are many pages written of my promises, and the fulfillment of many promises has come to pass. I will fulfill these promises in ways that you have no idea of because you have kept your hand in mine, your faith in mine, and called out to the Lord even for help in the times of storm, so I am the Lord God today that is with you.*

### *YOU ARE BLESSED...*

I have given to you those to stand by you in prayer. You are blessed unto the Lord. This day you are standing before me, saith God.

The things that have been hindering you in your life are going to be taken from you and unwrapped, so to speak, even as Lazarus. Even though he was resurrected by the power of my Word, yet by the same token he stood there bound, saith the Lord.

You have been bound because satan has kept you bound, and yea, you have seen this. So I am coming, and I have those around about you that will help to unwind all of these cloths, so to speak, that satan has put around you, the barriers, and the briers, and the bramble bushes.

I am the Lord God that sees you, and you will come forth. You are being called forth even now, and the devil is being called to a halt, saith the Lord.

Even as you lose yourself in prayer you are going to find yourself anew and afresh with the Lord your God. Many things are going to begin to happen that will show you that I am moving in a different direction even, saith God.

### *TAKE MY HAND...*

My mighty hand is outstretched to you, my child, for I am the unlimited God, saith the Lord. You have sought Me and I have heard your prayers. I have called out to you in the night-time and you have heard Me, saith God.

You have said in your heart, "Lord, I feel you. I feel you ministering to me. I feel you casting out the devil." I am the Lord God that has come to your rescue many, many times.

*I have not brought you this far in your journey, or out of the hardness of the streets, nor out of the darkness of the hallways, to let you perish, saith the Lord. But I am the Lord God that has brought you out into a land flowing with milk and honey.*

*You are coming into that land where you will see the grapes and the pomegranates that grow large. A new land, saith the Lord.*

*Be strong and be filled with courage, for I will always stand by you, saith God.*

## I LOVE YOU...

*I am God, and I will take the loneliness from you. I am the Lord God that will take fear from you. Cast your care upon the Lord for I care for you, and I love you, saith the Lord.*

*I love you as a husband.*

*I love you as a father, a mother.*

*I am your comforter.*

*Yea, behold! I am the Lord God that binds up the wounds. I am the Lord God that is saying to you tonight that you will be the one who will receive the benefits from all the prayers that you have prayed, for you are on the receiving end, saith God.*

*Bless the Name of the Lord, for you are on the receiving end of the things that you have asked Me for throughout the years. You are going to see that I am going to give you an outstanding and happy life ahead.*

*Hold on to the Lord your God for it is just around the corner, saith God.*

## SEEK THE LORD...

He that seeks the Lord finds the Lord, my children. As you seek the Lord over your trials and as you seek the Lord over your tribulations, then you will find Me ever ready to move for you and to remove the obstacles from your lives, saith the Lord.

I am the Lord God that loves you this day even as I love this great universe that I created. Are you not a part of that great universe?

My child, you shine like a star, a golden star. I have set you as a jewel that is set in a crown. Yea, a special large jewel, saith the Lord, in the position that you now hold.

You are going to see Me move in your life, saith God.

## PUT ON THE ARMOR...

My child, saith the Lord, the armor of the Lord is always around about you. Do not go by feelings whether or not you are really saved for you have been brought with the blood of Jesus Christ.

And you know in your heart, regardless of whether you are sick or well, young or old, rich or poor, that the Word of God stands faithful and true, saith the Lord.

Regardless of how you feel satan would make you feel that the armor of God was not there, the Lord God would say to you I was with David, armor or no armor, to protect him.

I am your Rock, your Sword, and your Shield! Yea, I am your Buckler, and a mighty strong Tower! I am, saith the Lord, the strength of your life.

You are saved by the Blood of Jesus Christ, and I have this day placed a golden banner over you, and yea satan dares not touch you.

*And the Lord God saith, you are only human, and to be drained is to know that the Spirit of the Lord was used in and through you. But I have built you back up again even though satan would say, "The armor of the Lord has not been around you or with you."*

*But yea, it is there, saith the Lord, because I am your Sword. I am your Shield, I am your Buckler.*

*Praise the Lord!*

### KEEP GOING...

*My child, you have weathered many a storm. But the best years of your life are still ahead. Even though you cannot see that now, or think it now, trust in me and believe in the Bible and the Words of God, and you will know that this is so.*

*For even though there are trials and tribulations for all My people, and many are the tribulations of the righteous, I say to you now that I will make a way through it all.*

*And now this day, saith God, My hand is upon you to encourage you in all that you have set your hand to do. For I have set you in a high place and you are doing a beautiful job of what I have set for you to do, saith the Lord.*

*Wait on the Lord; be of good courage, and He shall strengthen thine heart; wait I say, on the Lord. (Psalm 28:18 KJV)*

*For six days the cloud covered the mountain, and on the seventh day the Lord called to Moses from within the cloud. (Ex. 24:16 NIV)*

God created the heavens and the earth in six days (Gen 1:31)

Israel marched around Jericho six times (Josh 6:3)

**Dear Simon,**

When you called today to tell me you had broken your leg, I felt so sorry for you. I've never broken a bone so I don't know how that feels. But when you told me about how your family laughed and made fun of your predicament and how much that hurt you, I thought, *I know how that feels.*

My heart's been broken, several times in fact. So I can say to you, "I know how *that* hurts." I know the feelings of emptiness, loneliness, and rejection. I know what the ache in your heart felt like. I know the feeling of incompleteness, of nowhere to go, and no one to care. And you know that I know and why.

I've been through this valley of tears and I can tell you what I have learned. There is someone who has gone down this road ahead of you.

He has already made a path and he is waiting with outstretched arms, like a parent to a child, to lead you out of the darkness of the valley into the light of the mountaintop. His name is Jesus, and He loves you. Trust Him, like a child trusts his parent.

When your son gets in a tough spot and you say, "Here son, grab a hold of my hand and I'll help you up," he doesn't stop to mull it over in his mind (like what will people think). He reaches out in the simple faith of a child in his father, knowing beyond a shadow of a doubt that you will help him over the rough spot, or lift him up from where he has fallen, and set him on his feet.

That's all Jesus asks you to do...trust Him...take His hand and let Him prove Himself to you.

He *is* real. I know...I've met Him.

I found out He knows what a broken heart feels like.

I found out He knows how it hurts to be rejected.

I found out He knows what it is to be lonely, unloved, and unwanted.

And in my deepest hours of grief and despair, I know what it feels like to be lifted up onto that mighty lap and feel the arms of love around me, to feel the peace that passes all understanding fill my being till I know that I know that I know *He is*, and He cares for me.

And it's because I've been on that lap and felt those arms around me that I can tell *you*...He's real.

He'll fill your needs. He'll turn on the light. He'll give you peace. Just trust Him.

This message is so important to you the Lord won't let me back off from telling you. He is reaching out to you so strongly because He knows what you need. To be the vessel through which He can pour out His love to you is a feeling indescribable.

He loves you...He really does.

This great God of the universe knows you by name.

Love,
Mary M

PS: I'm still praying for you

## AND THE LORD SAID:

### I AM WITH YOU...

*I am the Lord that is with you in peculiar ways. I am the Lord that is the mender of broken hearts. I am the Balm of Gilead. And the Balm of Gilead will be applied, and is being applied, to your wounded heart right now, saith the Lord.*

*Yea, and I say to you, this wound has been broken open, and it is a serious wound, a wound that has been so painful and slow to heal, and is injurious. But I say to you today, I am the Lord God that is going to catch you away to a high place, and you will know that I took and sewed it up, so to speak, and mended your broken heart, saith God.*

*Therefore you will have the strength to go on, and you will have the power from God on high. For I am stitching in to that wounded place love and wisdom, understanding, and a depth of My Spirit that you never would have known if you had not suffered this, saith the Lord.*

### I WILL STRENGTHEN YOU...

*Yea, behold! I am the Lord that strengthens you in this hour. I am the Lord that still saith to you, I will keep every promise to you. For you will not have suffered this in vain, for I did not suffer on the cross in vain, saith the Lord.*

*Yea, people thought I did, but I did not for I rose victorious, and you are going to rise victorious with the healing Balm of Gilead in your wings, and upon My Spirit, and upon your spirit this day.*

*The Holy Spirit has come and united us as never before because you are My child, saith Jesus Christ of Nazareth, and I am your God, saith the Lord.*

### YOU ARE IN MY HAND...

*You are in the Hand of the Lord. I have been with you through the heartaches and the tears. I have beheld your every teardrop, and many times as you did cry, my heart was grieved, saith the Lord.*

*Even as I have said in My word, "I laugh with My people," by the same token, saith the Lord, by your every tear and your every teardrop, I cry.*

*Therefore, the many tears that you have shed I will recompense you with happiness, and you are coming into that happiness. Your laughter has been fuller for I have beheld you, and this is like stepping stones leading up to the very place where you are going to be elevated. And even now there is just a thin veil separating you from the promises that I have made you, saith the Lord.*

## HOLD ON...

*Hold on, saith the Lord. Yea, be full of joy! Yea, for I say to you that this is the joy of the Lord that's in your heart, and this is where your strength is coming from.*

*I am your healer.*

*I am your leader.*

*I am your guide.*

*And I say to you that great will be your happiness in the years to come, and the latter days of your life will be the opposite of anything you have ever known in your former days, saith the Lord.*

## I SEE YOUR TEARS

*Behold! I say to you at this hour I see your tears. And yea, your tears are bottled in heaven, saith the Lord.*

*Therefore, the time is drawing short even in heaven when the tears of My people, yea, My saint's bottles will be turned upside down and the tears will be sprinkled on the hearts and the lives of people, and the Lord will behold you anew and afresh, saith God.*

*There is power in your tears. Power and reminder of your grief and your broken heart.*

*Therefore, take courage today and stand tall. Take courage today and know that your life is being felt for the Lord, and you have stood up and been counted even on God's side, saith the Lord.*

## ANGELS ARE MINISTERING...

*I am blessing you and My Angels are ministering to you. You are feeling the relaxation of the ministering Angels. Therefore, even as you sleep I will whisper in your ear. When you awake on the morrow the many thoughts and the many divine interpretations that come to you will be because I talked to you tonight as you slept, saith the Lord.*

*I am strengthening you and I am under girding you with My power to do the work that you have to do, physically, mentally, and not only that but the spiritual warfare that you are in that drains you, saith God.*

*I am ministering to you along these lines, saith the Lord.*

## WALK IN PEACE...

*Yea, My child, you do have the peace of God Almighty. Yea, I have give you this peace, and the peace that you have I shall not take away.*

*It has come to you because you have prevailed and obeyed the Lord yea, to the very enth degree, and to the best of your ability, which is a high mark in God's sight, saith the Lord.*

*I am dealing with this man and time alone will tell, because you know yourself that it is according to a person's will what they will be, whether they will serve me, or whether they will not, saith the Lord.*

*Meanwhile, I have given you a peace that passes understanding. I have given you this peace and you have the respect of those around about you. Everyday that respect and the abilities that you have are more recognizable, at your job and at home with your family, saith the Lord.*

They respect you and look up to you which is a great reward and a great recompense yea, to the peace that you have found and you are indeed a minister in the sight of the Lord, saith God.

## STUDY THE WORD...

My daughter, you have studied and you have been lost in the words of God. Many times I have seen you as you have been rightly dividing the Word of God which so many people do not do, saith the Lord. They do not rightly divide the Word of God.

So therefore, this day I am with you to bless you and encourage you, to help you and to draw you closer to Me for I am an ever present help in the time of trouble, and this is troubled water, saith the Lord.

Therefore rejoice this day and look up, for I am with you to lead you into higher heights and deeper depths in the days to come. And if you keep your eyes open and your eyes on the Lord, you will see a great transformation in your whole life, even more than ever, to bring to pass all the promises that I have given you, saith the Lord.

> He healeth the broken in heart, and bindeth up their wounds. (Psalm 147:3 KJV)

# SEVEN

*By the seventh day God had finished the work He had been doing:*
*so on the seventh day He rested from all His work.  And God blessed*
*the seventh day and made it Holy, because on it He rested from all*
*the work of creating that He had done. (Gen. 2:2-3 NIV)*

His Word is as silver purified by fire seven times (Ps 12:6)
There are seven miracles in the Gospel of John
He shed His blood seven times for us
John wrote to the seven churches (Rev. 1:4)
Seven stars in Christ's hand (Rev 1:16)
Seven angels pronounce judgment in the Tribulation (Rev. 8:2)

**Dear Simon,**

I woke up last night thinking about bandages. What a powerful medicine bandages are. Remember as a child what a wonder-working thing a bandage was? When Mom put a bandage on an "owie" it was an "instant cure-all."

Even as adults, even though we no longer believe in its miracle working power, we try to apply some form of 'bandage' to ease our pain. For some it's booze. For some it's making money, or buying houses and cars. For some it's sex.

Your phone call yesterday made me think of a bandage. And even though it's too little, too late, your attempt to ease my hurt (or sooth your conscience) really touched my heart.

But how can you put a bandage on a broken heart? How can you tape up an image of a man that has fallen and been broken into a million pieces? You can't keep anyone on a pedestal with bandages, anymore than getting drunk or spending lots of money can cause a problem to go away.

Why, when you know that I know what I know, do you ask me to accept you as before, as though nothing is wrong?

It isn't me that needs the bandage Simon, it's you. But how do you put a bandage on a guilty conscience?

I have a new love now. His name is Jesus. With His help I have swept up all the broken pieces, dug a big hole, and buried them. There is nothing left to patch up for me, but maybe I can help you. May I try?

Your conscience is troubled...so here's my bandage.

Simon, I forgive you. In fact, I forgave you a long time ago. You just have never accepted it.

Consider this...have I ever yelled, or screamed, or cursed you?

Have I ever done anything to make you feel like you weren't welcome?

Have I ever put you down, betrayed you to your friends, lied to you, picked fights...or hurt you with words?

A bitter person cannot be a forgiving person, and there is no bitterness in my heart. Just hurt.

Deep down you really know this. You think you need to do something to earn my forgiveness, but you don't. You can't. It's yours...unconditionally...no strings attached.

Forgiveness is a bridge. It crosses deep chasms. But it must be a two-way bridge...so therefore I ask for your forgiveness.

Whatever I have done to hurt you, please forgive me.

Maybe my 'bandage' is small, but I offer it to you with all my heart...because I care about you, and I know that you care too.

I love you Simon and want you to know
I forgave you the hurts a long time ago.
But it's not my intention that you should feel blame
For the shame that I brought upon my own name.
Bargain basements for bargains, things that are cheap,
Things from the gutters, things from the streets.
The saying is true, "By your actions you're known,"
It really hit hard, it really hit home.
Now I ask your forgiveness, and pray that some day
You'll be able to 'see me' in a new way.
Just remember I love you, remember I care.
Whatever your need, I'll always be there.

Sincerely,
Mary M

PS: You are in my prayers

# AND THE LORD SAID:

### GO FORWARD

*I will always instruct you in the way you should go. I will answer your prayers because you have purposed in your heart to go forward and not backward. Because you have made this great decision in your life, you've become My child, saith the Lord. Therefore, even to the scriptures that I have given to you, you can stand upon the promises of God and the Word of the living God.*

### HOLD YOUR HEAD HIGH...

*You are a daughter of Zion. You are a daughter of the Most High King, clothed with golden cloth. You can hold your head high for I have also adorned your head with a crown of gold, saith the Lord.*

*Behold, no man or no weapon can ever stand before you because I am the King of Kings and you are a princess of the princesses.*

*As you meditate upon the Lord day and night, and as you are striving to do abundantly more than I've even asked of you in order for a soul to be saved, I am bringing this closer and closer to a climax, in ways that you know not of at this time, saith God.*

*Remember the times I have told you this? And remember this, that I not only have crowned you with a crown, but I will crown you with many more crowns, and the ones for whom you have prayed, saith the Lord.*

### PRAISE ME...

*In your praises, saith the Lord, is my joy fulfilled. And your joy is fulfilled because I've said the joy of the Lord is your strength.*

You will know the joy in time to come over the prayers you've prayed tonight, saith the Lord. Therefore take heed of this and know your God's eyes and ears are open unto your prayers.

**THERE WILL BE FIERY TRIALS...**
Think it not strange concerning your fiery trials. But rejoice this day in the midst of all your teardrops. In the mist of all your pain of heart, I the Lord thy God has seen that you outwardly praise me when inwardly your broken heart would almost overcome thee, saith the Lord.

But I, the Lord thy God, hold a hugh eraser in my hand that is able to erase all things from the memory of people. Therefore take heart and be full of courage and know that all the prophecies and all the promises, saith the Lord, are coming to pass.

**I AM HONORING YOU...**
Thou hast come a long way with your God and you are honored in the sight of the Lord because you're constantly remembering the words that I've said unto thee, saith the Lord.

Thou hast constantly been abiding, yea even as Mary, thinking upon the words that the Holy Spirit said unto her, and you have been doing likewise lo, these many years.

Just remember my child, you do not have to bow and scrape to anybody because you have the Savior on your side, saith God. You are there on the Cross of Calvary and you don't have to come down into any part of all the dirt because you are lifted up high.

Keep full of faith and courage because I am standing by you, saith the Lord, and you are standing by me.

## ONE STEP AT A TIME...

My child, you have grown! You have grown one step at a time. And as you have taken new fresh steps, sometimes you have taken a step in fear and trembling. But as you placed your foot more firmly, one foot ahead of the other, that foot would come down more firmly, and then you would feel the power of the Lord and the security of your God. And I would stand helping you. And the Angels were helping you!

So it will be all the days of your life. One step after another. You are growing and growing, and your steps are becoming longer and growing in length and breadth until, saith the Lord, you no longer tremble and are fearful, for you have this security.

I have placed a security guard around about you that would keep you and bless you and help you lest you should slip and fall. For I have ordained that you would be raised up even as a priestess would be raised up in the middle of her family yea, as a mighty warrior even.

So this day you know that God has answered your prayers in many ways. You know that all the things that I have promised you have not yet come to pass, but I would encourage you today to praise my name and believe. For surely as the sun comes up and the moon comes up and goes down, saith the Lord, the things I have promised you will come to pass.

> The name of the Lord is a strong tower; the righteous runneth into it, and is safe. (Proverbs 18:10 KJV)

# EIGHT

*And beside all this, giving all diligence, add to your faith (1) virtue (2) and to virtue knowledge (3) and to knowledge temperance (4) and to temperance patience (5) and to patience godliness (6) and to godliness brotherly kindness (7) and to brotherly kindness charity (8) (2 Peter 1:5-7)*

# ONE LAST THOUGHT. . .

I am 70 years old now. I have married, borne and raised children, kept a home, all the while working out of the home, and divorced. I have buried my only sibling (too young) my parents, and my children's Father.

If there's anything I have learned from my 70+ years it's that we are all 'Valley Walkers'. Broken hearts, broken dreams, and broken lives. Some valleys are deeper and darker than others, some longer and never seem to end. But, Praise God, one day you wake up and realize that you made it through and healing can begin.

One thing the Lord tells us to do is to 'comfort others as we are comforted" and that is the reason for this little book. Stories and thoughts. Prophecies, poems and dreams. Drawn from a lifetime of living not only from myself, but from family and friends, this anointed book is written simply to help you, the reader, through your valleys.

I still have a few more things in my folder and maybe some day the Lord will show me something else He wants me to do with them.

But in the meantime, I pray that what the Holy Spirit has revealed in these pages will lead you on to higher heights and deeper depths as you climb up the Golden Ladder from Glory to Glory.

So I leave you with one final prophecy...

# AND THE LORD WOULD SAY TO YOU. . .

*For yea, saith thy God unto thee My little children, the Lord loveth thee, yea. I have called unto thee to do a work for Me in this last and dying hour.*

*Behold as I was with Moses, I am with thee. As I fed Elijah and sustained him, I shall feed and sustain thee. So fear thee not.*

*Behold! Thou shall find a place by Me, a new hiding and abiding place, saith God. I am leading thee in new paths, as thou dost start for thy God.*

*I shall bless thee and in turn thou shalt bless and help My people.*

*Thou shalt teach, exhort, and manifest the gifts of the Spirit, magnifying the Name of Jesus, the Christ, whom thou lovest.*

*Amen and Amen*


Even so, Lord Jesus, Come.

# MAKE A DECISION

## HOW TO RECEIVE JESUS AS THE LORD AND SAVIOR OF YOUR LIFE

Romans 10:9 states, *that if you confess with your mouth, "Jesus is Lord," and believe in your heart that God raised Him from the dead, you will be saved.*

It's really that simple. Don't worry about all the baggage that you carry around. Don't stop to 'wash your hands' as it were. Just come to the foot of the cross, accept Jesus as your Lord and Savior and He will take care of the cleanup details.

> *For it is with your heart that you believe and are justified, and it is with your mouth that you confess and are saved. (Romans 10:10 NIV)*

The next step is to say it out loud, "confess with your mouth"... just repeat this simple prayer.

"Jesus, I believe in my heart that you are the Son of God. That you died and arose on the third day for my sins. I confess with my mouth that I am a sinner and I need your love and forgiveness. I want to be a new person and have life eternal. I confess you now as my Lord and Savior. Please come into my life, cleanse me and make me free. Thank you, Jesus, for saving my soul."

If you repeated that prayer you are now a new creation! Get a Bible and start spending time with Jesus. Thank Him at the beginning of each new day for His protection and love. Daily, ask Him to guide your steps in the way you should go.

If you don't have a church home, look for a Bible believing church, introduce yourself to the Pastor, and tell him you are a new Christian and he will help you with your new life in Christ.

Praise the Lord! See you in heaven!

*For God so loved the world that he gave His only begotten Son, that whosoever believeth in Him should not perish, but have everlasting life. (John 3:16)*

To order additional copies of

# VALLEY WALKERS

have your credit card ready and call
1 800-917-BOOK (2665)

or e-mail
orders@selahbooks.com

or order online at
www.selahbooks.com

Printed in the United States
222132BV00004B/1/P

9 781589 302297